His Eyes Were Raining

Eric King Collins

Published by Pecan Tree Publishing
January 2022
Hollywood, FL
www.pecantreebooks.com
adminservices@pecantreebooks.com

979-8-9855014-3-8   Paperback
979-8-9855014-4-5   E-book
Library of Congress Control Number: 2022900922

Original Illustrations by: Donna Dodson, cadylikekatie@gmail.com
Cover and Interior Design by: faizandfx

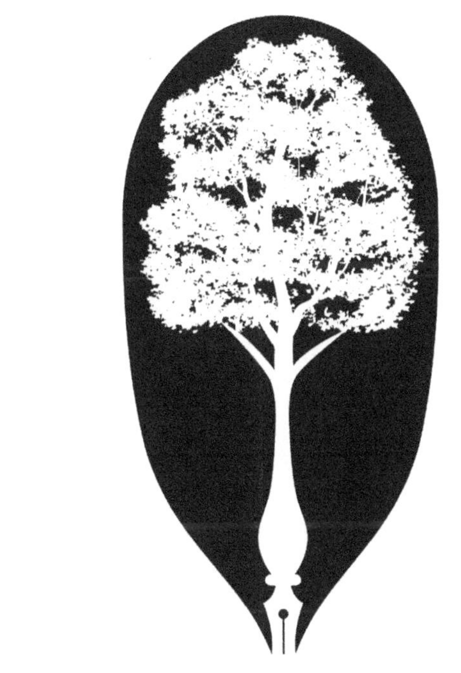

PECAN TREE

PUBLISHING

Acknowledgments

Thank you Cynthia D. Stargell for introducing me to E. Claudette Freeman of Pecan Tree Publishing. Pecan Tree Publishing has helped make a dream come true by bringing to life this story about the love of family.

I would like to thank my daughter, Candace for her Christian spirit, creative writing, and graphic gift.

Applause to Christine Nolan and her daughter, Syreeta Woodson, who were helpful in the initial editing process.

A special thanks to Donna Dodson for her patience, talent, and willingness to provide illustrations for this story.

The inspiration for this book comes from family members, foremost my father, Ernest Levi Collins, my mother, Ruby Collins and the mother of my daughters, Sandra Collins.

Most importantly, I thank God for giving me the vision to create this book to help children and families in the healing process of losing a loved one.

This book began as a high school first-year literature class assignment for my daughter Candace. Her task: write a narrative applying her five senses to create words that were descriptive. Candace wrote about her grandpa's funeral. She was nine years old when he passed away. This book was written to touch the lives of others in an unforgettable way. We acknowledge your grief and hold you in prayer.

A Note from the Author – Eric King Collins

This book began as a high school first-year literature class assignment for my daughter Candace. Her task: write a narrative applying her five senses to create words that were descriptive. Candace wrote about her grandpa's funeral. She was nine years old when he passed away. When my daughter shared her story with me, I thought the story should be shared with close friends who had lost a loved one. Over the years the story has been edited and transformed to become a book to touch the lives of others in an unforgettable way.

As a young man I found myself seeking ways to support others. As an adult I gravitated toward helping professions ranging from foster care work to varying fields of education. My family's vision for this book is to remind us all that whatever life brings our way, God is still in control. Through it all God is still blessing us.

"When I was a child, I talked like a child, I thought like a child, I reasoned like a child. When I became a man, I put the way of childhood behind me. For now, we see only a reflection as in a mirror, then we shall see face to face." First Corinthians 13:11-12 (Easy English Bible)

I know how it feels to lose someone or something really important. I lost my grandpa. He was my Superman! He was strong, confident, and kind. I called grandpa Superman because he never complained when he was sick.

Grandpa was always singing a happy tune. I enjoyed going on fishing trips and traveling to family reunions with him.

He always smelled like peppermint candy and his sweet blend of pipe tobacco. Grandpa was always there for me.

When he died, I did not feel like anything would help my pain go away. I felt small and confused. I could not figure out where the hurt in me was coming from. My dad saw my sadness and asked, "Dear heart, how are you feeling today? Do you understand what has happened to your grandpa and why he is no longer here?" I nodded yes. Dad said," You can always come to me or your mom or anyone in the family if you need to talk."

My father is a strong man. He is like a superhero for God. Even when grandpa died, he still believed in God with everything he had! My dad is a lot like his father. He is always here for me. To me, he resembles a great oak tree. My dad might bend and sway when the winds of life blow, but he never breaks or falls. My dad is no softy; and I never saw him cry - except for one day. It's surprising how a person can change when they lose a person they love.

I remember the day of my grandpa's funeral. That was the day we all had to say good-bye. I sat on one side of the bed and watched my legs dangle in the air. When my feet hit the cold and chilly floor, it made me jump.

I peered out the window. Everything looked sad and gray.
The birds were not singing. The sun was not shining. They
were sad that grandpa was gone too.

That morning I did not smell the aroma of bacon, ham, or eggs cooking in the kitchen. There was no bread browning in the toaster oven. No one was sitting at the table.

When I walked into the living room, I saw my grandma sitting in my grandpa's easy chair. She was ready to go to church. Everything was in place: from her hat and coat, all the way down to her shoes. In her right hand was her cane. Lying beside her was her purse and Bible.

Grandma lifted her head to look at my face. She smiled and said, "Good morning. Did you sleep well?"

Then my dad entered the room. While fixing his tie he looked at me with surprise. He said, "I know you want to spend some time with your grandma but get ready first. In one hour, a car is coming to pick the family up to take us to the church."

I ran into the bathroom, showered, and washed my face really good. I almost tore my stockings trying to hurry. I didn't want to keep everyone waiting. Once I finished dressing, I ran into the living room.

Each face I saw above me looked pale, emotionless, lost, and dazed. Their insides must have hurt like mine. We formed a circle, held hands, and prayed. During the prayer, I lifted my bowed head and tried to understand what was going on. It did not feel the same without grandpa there. My great-aunt said, "Amen," and then we were out the door to church.

The misty rain was chilly and damp. The sound of the car's windshield wipers going back and forth almost lulled me to sleep. My mind was clouded with so much confusion. There was no room for dreaming.

When we got out of the car at the church, I grabbed my father's hand. The tighter I squeezed his hand the more comfortable I felt. When we walked inside the church, my whole body went numb. If dad had let go of my hand, oh, boy, I don't think I could have walked to my seat. The church felt strange. I don't know why. I had visited many times.

Once I had settled myself down and looked at the church's towering walls, I felt safe. I could feel the warmth and peace of friends and family embracing my soul.

The pastor began the service. Right before my father and his brother went up to speak, a close friend of my mom's quietly asked my mother, "Do you want me to take the baby?" My sister was barely one year old. My mom nodded her head yes and handed my sister to her. My mother pulled me next to her. I think she found comfort in my sister and me. I looked at my grandma and thought she must have felt the same as my mother as she looked at her children. My grandparents had three children. There was one girl and two boys. Their daughter died soon after she was born. That left my uncle, who was the oldest, and my father, who is ten years younger than him.

My father got up from his seat and the entire church seemed to grow calmer. I don't remember paying attention to anyone else the whole service, but when my father spoke, my eyes were locked on him. At that moment, I could not see anyone but him. His words were straight from his heart. Then something strange happened.

While my dad was talking, I began to hear my grandfather's voice! I glanced over at the church pew where grandpa usually sat. I squinted my eyes. It was if I could see grandpa sitting there. I could hear him singing the song, "I will trust in the Lord until I..." Then, right before I let grandpa finish the next phrase of the song, I glanced upon my father's face.

My father looked up from his paper and took a deep breath.
His eyes began to rain. The more his eyes rained, the more
my heart sank. I asked my mom, "Why is dad crying?"

Mom replied in a quiet, gentle voice, "When God took your grandpa home to glory, that special place in heaven; grandpa left all his pain on earth. Your grandpa suffered from a sickness called cancer." She paused, and then told me, "The Lord's grace and mercy freed your grandpa from all the burdens of this world."

My mother smiled as her eyes rained softly, "Today your grandpa's tears fell from your father's eyes. All your grandpa's family and friends share those tears. The tears cleanse our minds and our hearts, and nourish our souls.

I said to my mom, " So our tears are like rain."

Mom said, "You've got it. I'm so proud of you." She gave me a big hug and I felt better.

Do you know what I learned when grandpa died? That through the storms, God's love, can catch all the rain that falls from our eyes and our hearts. And He can use the rain to help us grow.

Share this book with those who have lost a loved one.

Think of good memories of your loved one that have passed on and write those thoughts down to comfort you:

____

____

____

____

____

____

____

____

____

____

____

____

____

____

____

____

____

____